Oops! *Your meatball flips off your fork and onto Mrs. Sneeden's tablecloth.*

Gulp! *You've got six friends, but Mom says you can invite only three to your party.*

Wow! *You're invited to the fanciest wedding on earth. You want to behave perfectly but aren't sure you know how.*

Dear Reader,

You're getting older. You're going new places and doing new things. You have more independence, and more responsibility, too. Suddenly everybody expects you to act more like an adult—and less like your little sister. But that's not always easy to do.

Manners can help. Manners are a common-sense guide to getting along with other people. They prevent you from being selfish or annoying. They remind you to be kind. They make you better company—and a better person. A girl with nice manners gets respect because she gives it. She's also got the tools to handle all kinds of situations. She finds confidence she never knew she had.

This book describes the basic manners all girls need. We hope you enjoy *Oops!* We hope you use what you learn here, too. Every girl has what it takes to wow the world. Manners can help you do just that.

Your friends at American Girl

Contents

A big "sorry" cleaned
up this mess.

Doggie's first walk.
WHOA! "Excuse us, please!"

"Can I help?" The start
of a great friendship.

I've learned
all that.
What's next?

Word Watch

Manners are a kind of code. You use the code to let people know you're kind and respectful. At the same time, others read the code to decide what they can expect from you. *Can I trust this girl to treat me well? Does she think only about herself? Would she make a good friend or a poor one?* People look at your manners and make up their mind.

It's all about communication, and communication starts with words.

The words you choose

Before you start using a word, ask yourself: Is this word saying what I want it to say? Or might it be saying something altogether different?

Putdowns

Many girls use putdowns when they're kidding around with their friends. "It's just a joke," they say. "No one's hurt." Maybe. But a putdown always makes another person feel just a l-i-t-t-l-e dumber than she did before you said it. Putdowns *sting*. Maybe a bit. Maybe a lot.

The way you say them

Of course, pleasant words don't count if the tone of your voice says "I don't mean what I'm saying."

I'm sorry.

SORRY!!

Huh?

Hmm, eh, mmm, nah, yeah, huh. We all use these words sometimes, but it's a bit like wearing pajamas to school. It's lazy. Worse, it gives the impression that you dragged yourself out of a deep sleep to have this conversation—and wish you were still in bed.

Swearing

Swear words give your speech a sharp, nasty flavor. They make other people draw away as if they'd bitten into something bitter.

The company you're in

Chances are, the way you talk with a good friend when you're flopped on the grass is very different from the way you talk to the principal in the hallway at school. You change your style without thinking, almost like flipping a switch. And that's good.

Words that work with one kind of person often don't work with another. For instance, you and a close friend may use the word *duh* just in fun. But if you use *duh* with a kid you don't know very well, it's hurtful. And if you use it with an adult, it's insulting.

Body Language

You also send all sorts of messages with your body—with the way you stand and sit and walk. Want proof?

Look at the girls below and see if you can match each one with what she's saying with her body language.

1 I'm listening. I'm interested.

2 I'm so bored I'm wilting.

3 I'm mad and I'm not listening to a thing you say.

4 I'm glad to see you.

5 You are SO stupid.

Answers

1-d, 2-e, 3-a, 4-b, 5-c. Remember that the way you stand and sit says a lot. It's wrong to insult others in words. It's wrong to insult them with your body, too.

First Impressions

We all know we shouldn't judge a book by its cover. But the fact is that most of us *do* make judgments about others based on how they look and talk. This is especially true if we're meeting someone for the first time.

Don't let this business of appearances spook you. Instead, try out the tips on these pages. You'll *look* more confident, and that can often make you *feel* more confident, too. The more you practice these things, the more natural they'll feel. A little work on the outside girl lets the girl inside shine through—and *that,* of course, is the entire point.

"I'm ready for the world"

Your body says a lot about what you think about yourself. Take charge of your posture, and you're saying "I'm a girl who's ready for the world." Others will see you that way, too.

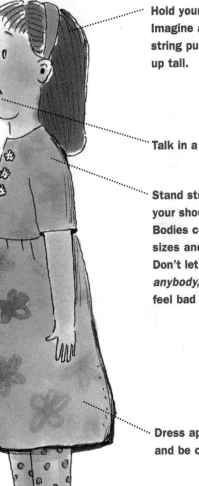

Hold your head up. Imagine an invisible string pulling you up tall.

Talk in a strong voice.

Stand straight with your shoulders back. Bodies come in all sizes and shapes. Don't let anybody, but *anybody,* make you feel bad about yours.

Dress appropriately, and be clean and neat.

Standing

If you stand in a slouch with your arms hugged across your chest, you look as if you're trying to fold up and disappear.

Walking

You're going somewhere in this world. Walk that way! Hold your head high and don't shuffle your feet.

Sitting

When it comes to sitting, try not to slump. Sit with your feet on the floor, your legs together, and your back straight.

That is, like, you know, like, really, like, cool.

Junk words

Junk words—such as *like* and *you know*—clog your sentences like goop clogs a sink. They make you sound stupid when you're not.

Nervous habits

Nervous habits tend to make other people nervous, too. Putting your hands in your pockets can help. So can lacing your fingers together in your lap.

Out of control

Puppies can get away with bounding around a room in a whirl of noise and chaos. Girls your age can't. If you feel yourself getting too excited, back away from the action. Sit down or go into another room till you feel calmer.

After You!

There are certain things people do that say "You're number one" or "Your needs come first." These actions are called signs of deference. They're rooted in tradition—and in kindness. Deference turns up in all sorts of ways in manners, but here are a few of the big ones.

Seats

If you're on a crowded bus or subway, you should give up your seat to anybody who looks as if he or she needs to sit down more than you do. This includes older people and people with babies or small children.

Guests first

Guests go first. When you're pouring lemonade, pour your friend's glass before you pour your own. When you start a game, let her have the first turn. And when there's only one cookie left . . . you know who gets it!

Men & women

Some manners stay the same from one generation to the next. Others change with the times. Often old rules and new ways live side by side.

For instance, women still get special treatment when it comes to manners: many men will hold a door open for a woman, and women are generally served first in restaurants and at parties. These traditions don't make much sense now that we all know men and women are equal. Lots of people keep them up anyway simply because they like them.

Hats

It's simply tradition: If your hat is part of a fancy outfit (say, an Easter bonnet), you can keep it on in the house. But it's hats off for baseball caps unless an adult tells you otherwise. Caps should *always* be off at dinner, and the same goes for hoods on jackets and sweatshirts.

Doors

Hold doors open for adults. When you and a friend are going through a doorway, let her go ahead of you.

The Golden Rule

There is a little imp inside us all that says, "Me first!" If "me first!" had its way, we'd all go through life bashing into one another's rights and feelings, and pretty soon the world would be a snarling mess.

Luckily, we have our manners. And manners remind us to put ourselves in the other guy's shoes.

Manners weren't invented by Fusspots, Inc. Most of them grew out of good old common courtesy. They're not just for adults but for your friends and family, too. They're not just for fancy occasions but for every day. The most important rule of all is the Golden Rule:

Do unto others as you would have them do unto you.

Greetings

Conversation. You use it to weave relationships with all sorts of other people. You want to be good at it—and you can be. It starts with a simple "Hi."

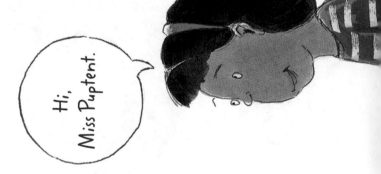

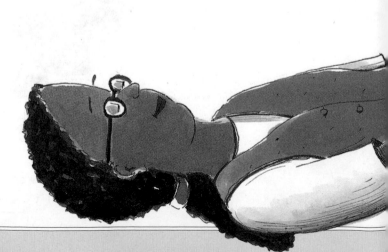

Say hello

Say hello to people you know. "Hi" means "I know you. I'm glad to see you, even if we're not going to stop and talk." Silence means . . . well, who knows? It might mean "I'm mad at you" or "I don't like you." And it definitely means "There you are, but so what?"

Use names

Greet people by name. It shows that you care who they are and makes them feel good.

If you have trouble remembering names, practice saying them when they're fresh in your mind. For instance, if you're being introduced to a new girl, say her name right away. (If you didn't quite catch it, ask her to repeat it till you do.) Then say her name several more times before the conversation's done. The more often you use the name today, the better chance you have of remembering it tomorrow.

Stand up

If you're greeting an adult, you should stand to say hello. Do you do this even if you've seen this person many times before? Yes. Even if your favorite TV show is on? Afraid so.

Eye contact

Look people in the eye. It shows that you're friendly and honest. It also tells others that you're interested in them and in what they're saying.

Shake hands

Step up and shake hands when you're saying hello to an adult, especially if the situation is fairly formal. Offer your right hand (even if you're left-handed) and say the person's name: "Hi, Miss Puptent." When she puts her hand in yours, clasp it firmly for one quick shake.

Introductions

If you find yourself with people who don't know each other, introduce them. If you don't, they'll sit there wondering, *Should I speak to that person or ignore him?* They'll feel awkward. So get the ball rolling by saying their names and offering a little information about each person. There are a few rules about how to do this, but if you forget the rules, it's not the end of the world. The worst goof is not to make the introduction at all.

Address a woman before a man.

Address the older person first.

Mrs. Mop, I'd like to introduce my friend Bitsy Broom.

Bitsy, Mrs. Mop works with my mom.

Rachel Rutabaga, I'd like to introduce my swim coach, Gus Grape.

Gus, Rachel used to babysit for me.

Identify the people you're introducing and use the names they'll use for each other.

Mrs. Squeamish, I'd like to introduce my cousin Squidge Mealy.

Squidge, Mrs. Squeamish is my neighbor.

An introduction is a good opportunity to let someone know that members of your family use different last names.

It's also a good way to identify stepparents:

But—yikes!—what if you forget someone's name completely? All is not lost. Introduce the person you *do* know, and chances are, the other one will finish the job for you by saying her name herself.

Mr., Ms., & More

Mr. and Ms. are among the most common titles people use to address one another, but there are many more in the deck. Mrs., Miss . . . if these terms are shuffled up in your brain, not to worry. Here's how to use them.

Mr.
A man

Mrs.
A married woman

Ms.
A woman, married or unmarried

Mr. & Ms.

A couple with different last names

Mr. & Mrs. or Mr. & Ms.

A couple with the same last name

Miss

A girl or an unmarried woman

Here's the deal

These days, many kids address adults by their first name. That's fine if the adult has invited you to do it. Until then, you should stick with Mr., Ms., Mrs., or Miss, depending on what the person prefers.

"Miss" isn't used as much as it used to be. Many people feel it's silly to identify women by whether or not they're married.

Boys used to be called "Master." These days, the only place you'll see "master" is in formal addresses on envelopes.

In some parts of the country, particularly the South, many people use "sir" and "ma'am" to show respect.

There are lots of special rules that apply to university professors, politicians, diplomats, royalty, religious leaders, and members of the military. So if you have some VIPs (some Very Important People) in your future, talk to an adult about how to address them.

Chitchat

It's not always easy to know what to say to keep a conversation going. But believe it or not, chatting is a lot like riding a bike, playing an instrument, or any other skill. The more you practice, the better you get.

Break the ice

You may be shy. You may have nothing to say. But if you stand silently beside another person, how is she to know you're not just unfriendly? Ask some questions: "When did you move in?" "Who's your teacher?" The more she talks, the more relaxed you'll *both* feel.

Take turns

A conversation is like a tennis match. You say something. The other person takes your thought and bops back one of her own. That's how it goes: back and forth, back and forth. If one or the other holds on to the ball and starts talking nonstop, the game's kaput.

Listen

We all like a good listener because she makes us feel that our thoughts and feelings matter. If you want to become a better listener, do this:

- Encourage the other person to talk by asking questions.
- Let her know you've heard what she's said by commenting on it.
- Don't always switch the subject back to yourself.

Interrupting

Wait till the other person stops talking before you start. If you want to drive somebody crazy— Drive somebody cra— If you want to drive somebody crazy— ARGH! ISAIDifyouwanttodrive somebodyCRAZY, interrupting is a good way to do it!

Zzzzz

If someone's boring you:
- Try to change the subject.
- Make a nice excuse. ("I'd better go to class." "I think I'll get a juice." "Guess I better leave now. See you soon!") Then make your escape.

But don't:
- Let your eyes wander around the room, looking for other people you'd rather be with.
- Say "Can we change the subject? This is boring."
- Walk off without saying anything.

If you want to avoid boring other people:
- Ask them questions.
- Talk about something other than yourself.
- Don't talk all the time.
- Don't tell really long stories, give really long speeches, or describe every little detail of a dream, TV show, or movie.

Oops!

What do you say when you don't know *what* to say?

Honesty?

Your brother's girlfriend walks in the door. Her hair is red. Yesterday it was blond—and looked a whole lot better. An obvious change in someone's appearance is like an elephant in the kitchen: it's just too big to ignore. But if you say what's in your mind, this girl will feel terrible. So make it short and sweet: "You changed your hair! You look nice." It's not right to lie, but sometimes it's better to leave a thought unsaid than to say it and hurt someone else.

Divorce

Jenna bursts into tears at lunch. Sobbing, she tells you, "My parents are getting divorced!"
Express your sympathy and concern ("I'm really sorry!"). Offer what help you can ("Can I take your tray back for you?" "You can come over to my house anytime"). If Jenna doesn't want to talk, leave her in peace. If she *does* want to talk, listen. Questions about her future are O.K. ("Do you know who you'll live with?" "Will you still come to this school?"). Prying into her parents' troubles is *not* O.K. ("What do they fight about?"). Finally, don't say anything bad about either of Jenna's parents—even if she does.

Hospital

Last night, your parents told you that your Uncle Lev is dying. Today you have to visit him in the hospital. "Hi, Kelcy," he says when you walk in. "How's my girl?" He's got tubes in his arms, he looks horrible, and you wish you were anywhere but here.

Hospital rooms make a lot of people feel like running for the car. Don't do it. Walk on in and say, "I'm doing fine, Uncle Lev. But I'm so sorry you're sick!" Ask questions about his daily comfort: "Are the doctors and nurses nice?" "Is there anything I can get for you?" If Uncle Lev brings up a subject, talk about that. If he doesn't, talk about one or two things going on in your life. The two of you may laugh—and that's great. Laughter can cheer things up and help you both relax. You may also cry. That's O.K., too. It's right to acknowledge powerful feelings, and to express fear and love. Stay a half hour or less, so you don't tire him out. Then you can head home with a full heart, knowing you did what you could to comfort your uncle when he needed it most.

Speaking up

Mr. and Ms. Burns are over for dinner after soccer. "The Hornets play dirty," Mr. Burns says to your dad. You've played against the Hornets, and you know this isn't true. Is it O.K. to speak up and say so?

Absolutely. Say "Mr. Burns, I don't agree. I've played the Hornets, and they were fine sports." Express yourself politely, but by all means *do* express yourself. It's not bad manners to share strong beliefs or opinions—especially when it comes to someone's honor and big issues of right and wrong.

Nosy Questions

When it comes to conversation, there are good questions and there are nosy questions. Good questions lead people to talk about things they want to talk about. Nosy questions embarrass them or make them uncomfortable. Do you know a nosy question when you see one? Find out. Read on and circle the questions that should not have been asked.

Be sure to respect other people's privacy on subjects relating to money, medical conditions, religion, an adult's age, and a person's looks. Most important, don't pry into sad or tragic situations.

Answers
O.K. questions: 2, 3, 4, 6, 11, 13, 16
Nosy questions: 1, 5, 7, 8, 9, 10, 12, 14, 15

Telephones

Making a call

Check the time before you make a call. If it's before nine in the morning or after nine at night, don't dial. People in the house may be asleep, even if your friend isn't. Avoid calling during the dinner hour, too.

When someone picks up, don't keep her guessing about who you are. Identify yourself.

If you call a wrong number, say, "I'm sorry. I think I have the wrong number. Is this 231-1111?" Don't just hang up. It's rude. Check to make sure you have the right number before dialing again.

Answering machines

Sometimes *(beep!)* an answering machine will take your call. Give your name, the time, and explain why you're calling: "Hi. This is Jenny Lind. I'm calling for Keisha about the picnic. It's about seven. Keisha, would you call me back, please? Thanks!"

34

Answering a call

Some parents think a simple "Hello" is fine. Others prefer children to answer by identifying the family: "Hello, Washbuckets' residence."

If the phone is for your brother Alfie, go find him to tell him about the call. *Don't* stand in the kitchen and holler, "ALFIE, PHONE'S FOR YOU." Or even worse: "IT'S THAT GIRL YOU DON'T LIKE. SHOULD I TELL HER YOU'RE NOT HERE?"

If a friend calls during dinner, tell her you're eating and will call back.

If you answer the phone and someone has dialed a wrong number, be polite about their mistake. But it's unsafe to give out your number, so if the caller asks for it, turn the question around. Say "What number did you dial?" If the number the caller gives isn't yours, say so. If it is, say simply, "That's our number, but there's no one here by that name."

Messages

Have you ever missed out on some fun with a friend because you didn't get the message when she called? Remember how that made you feel? *That's* why we should all jot down messages while we're still on the phone.

Don't be afraid to ask a caller to go slowly, repeat information, or spell a name. You're being careful, and the person will appreciate that.

Home alone

If you're home alone and a caller asks for one of your parents, don't say you're by yourself. Instead say, "I'm sorry. Mom can't come to the phone right now. May I take a message?"

Thursday, 4:15 —
Mom: Michelle
called. Call her
after 6 tonight.
555-4321

35

Talking on the phone

When you're on the phone, you should talk to the person on the other end. Not watch TV. Not read. And *definitely* not eat. (It's like chewing your food in someone's ear.)

Phones have to be shared. If you and your friend have been chatting for a half hour, it's time to get off.

May I PLEASE use the phone?

Call-waiting

When your family has call-waiting, don't ignore the beep. If the call coming in is more important than the call you're on, tell your friend you have to call her back later.

36

C'mon Over!

Life with Friends

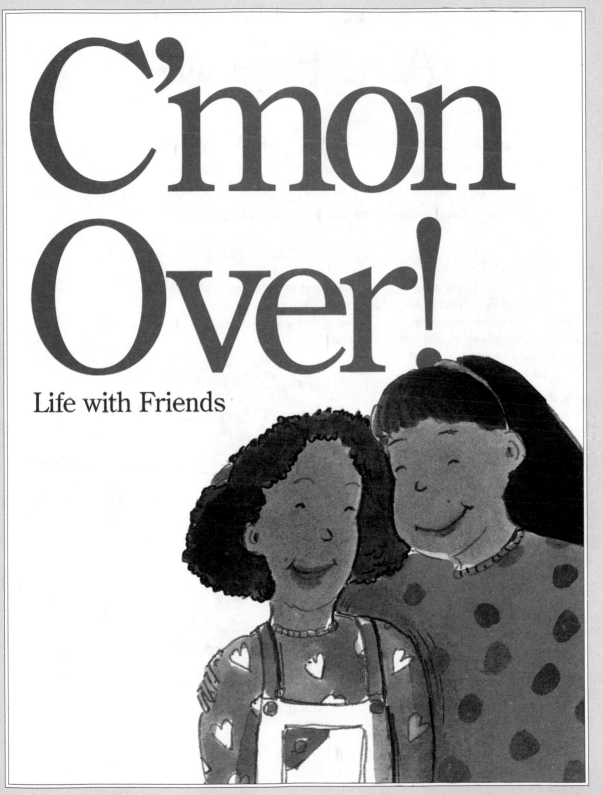

At a Friend's

You're getting together with a friend. Sounds like fun! If she's coming to your place, make her feel welcome and comfortable. If you're going to hers, be respectful of property and privacy. It's all part of being a good host and a good guest—and a thoughtful and considerate friend.

Being a host

Greet your guest at the door. Show her where to hang up her coat and stash her belongings. If she's never been to your home before, show her around and introduce her to your family.

Is there any special information your friend needs to know? Is the dog friendly? Is your mom's office off-limits? Clue her in so she'll know what to do—and what *not* to do.

Ask your guest if she'd like something to eat and drink. It's a good way to make her feel welcome.

Be flexible when it comes to what to do. Suggest several different activities and ask your friend for her suggestions, too. Pick something you're both happy with.

See your guest to the door when she leaves. If your parents are driving her home, go along in the car.

Being a guest

If your shoes are wet and dirty, take them off when you come in the door. Don't dump your coat and belongings in a heap on the floor or on a chair.

Be friendly to other people in the house. Greet them by name.

Don't wander around the house on your own. Stick with your friend and let her be the guide.

It's up to the host to offer food and drink. If you know your host well, it's O.K. to let her know you're hungry, but you should never help yourself.

Respect the belongings of the people in the house. Don't examine or use objects as if they were your own.

If you need to use the phone, ask first.

If you helped make a mess, be sure you help clean it up.

Say "Thank you" when you leave.

Sleepovers

Every household has its own habits and routines. When you're invited for a sleep-over, your job is to fit in and pitch in.

At **dinner** use good table manners and clear your place when you've finished eating. Help out in the kitchen and with any other chores your friend has to do.

Snooping is wrong. Don't open up drawers in a desk or dresser. Don't inspect cupboards and closets. Never, ever read diaries, letters, bills, or other papers—even if they're lying out on a counter or desktop.

The **bathroom** is a private place. If you want to be alone when you change clothes, that's the place to do it. Just don't stay in there too long, and be sure it's clean when you leave.

Use only the towel you're told to use. Rinse the sink out after you've brushed your teeth and wipe up any water on the countertop. When you've finished, fold your towel and hang it up.

Be quiet late at **night.** A girl who keeps sleepy people up at 2 A.M. is a girl who won't be invited back anytime soon.

But if you're ill, homesick, or scared, it's O.K. to turn to your friend or her parents for help. Manners don't require you to pretend you're all right when you're not!

Before you say **good-bye,** make sure you've made your bed. And remember to thank your friend and your friend's parents when you leave.

Oops!

Manners give you the skills you need to handle all sorts of situations that arise with friends.

Share or not?

You're at the mall with Tara. She just spent all her money on a headband at the drugstore. Three shops later, you decide to buy a bag of candy. Do you have to share?

It's impolite to eat in front of a person who doesn't have anything to eat herself. You don't have to give Tara half your candy, but you should offer her a few pieces.

Saying no nicely

The phone rings. It's Sophie. "Want to spend the night?" she asks. You don't want to hurt Sophie's feelings, but in your heart of hearts, you don't like her very much.

A friendly invitation deserves a friendly reply—even if the reply is no. So use the same tone of voice you would use for a girl you like a lot. Don't say anything hurtful, like "I don't want to be friends" or "Why are you calling me?" Thank Sophie for the invitation when you make your excuse: "I'm sorry, Sophie. I have plans. It was nice of you to ask me."

Borrowing

Valerie borrowed your favorite book five weeks ago. You really want it back. Ask her, in a friendly way, "Are you finished with the book?" If she says yes, ask how she liked it—and add, "Would you please bring the book to school tomorrow? I'd like to have it back." If she says no, give her a deadline: "I'd like to have it back by Tuesday, O.K.?" Then call Monday night to remind her.

Correcting friends

It's lunchtime. Your pal Mindy is eating with her mouth open. It's disgusting. Do you say something?

Mention it once or twice, in a kind and private way, then back off. It sounds as if Mindy could use some friendly advice, but it's not your job to police your friends.

R-r-ing!

You'd like to do your homework with Danielle. Can you walk to her house, or do you have to call first?

Call first. Danielle might love to see you, but she might also be doing something with another friend. By calling, you make it easier for Danielle to say no if she wants to. You also avoid creating a situation that could be awkward for you both.

Big news

You're so excited! You've been given two tickets to the concert you and Min-ha have *dreamed* about. You find her in the hallway, talking to Anna. This is big news! Do you tell her now?

No. You and Min-ha get to do something special, and that's great. But if Anna isn't going to be included in the fun, it's rude to talk about it in front of her. This news can wait, and it should.

Invitations

Hooray! It's party time. And a good party starts with a good invitation. Invitations should be mailed at least a week and a half before the big event. Be sure to tell your guests everything they need to know.

What
What sort of party is it?

Who
Who's giving the party? (You, of course!)

When & where
When and where will the party take place?

Special info
Is there anything special your guests should know?

Reply
R.S.V.P. is short for the French phrase *Répondez s'il vous plaît* (reh-pon-day seel voo play). It means "Reply if you please." A guest who receives an invitation saying R.S.V.P. should tell the host as soon as possible whether or not she can come.

It's a Summer Birthday Splash!

who: Wendy Waters
Day: Saturday, July 14
Time: 11:00-2:00
Where: Lakewood Public Pool

Bring a towel and swimsuit. (We'll bring everyone home afterward.)

R.S.V.P. 231-1234

Oops!

Uninvited

What do you do if you see someone handing out invitations and she doesn't give you one?

Very hurt

Invitations should be mailed or delivered to homes, not handed out at school in front of girls who aren't invited. When you're left out in this inconsiderate way, you may be tempted to confront the host and ask, "Why didn't you ask me?" or "Can I please come anyway?" Don't. It will only make you feel worse. Instead, find a friend. Talking and laughing with another girl can help you hide your embarrassment and soothe hurt feelings. Remind yourself that the person who's done something she should be ashamed of is the host—not you.

Only three

Once a girl invited me to her birthday party. When my birthday came around, I could invite only three people. I picked my three closest friends, and she was not one of them. She was very upset. I felt so bad. Was that the right thing to do?

Kelly

When a friend invites you to her birthday party, it's nice to return the favor by inviting her to yours. But if you've been to a lot of birthday parties and can have only three guests to yours, you'll need to find other ways to express your friendship. If you know you're going to leave a friend out, invite her to a movie or a sleepover on another day. Honesty is a good idea, too. Getting left out is never fun, but if a girl knows that your mom set a limit on guests, the news might be a whole lot easier to take.

Oops!

Guest vs. guest

I invited this girl to a party. Now another girl says she won't come if that girl does. What should I do?

In the middle

Tell the girl who's threatening to skip your party that you aren't going to change your guest list for her. A good guest tries to get along with other guests whether she likes them or not. And she doesn't bully the host, either.

No-shows

I planned a party and all 12 people said they could come, but only nine showed up.

Erika

For every girl who doesn't show up when she says she will, there's an empty chair, an extra treat bag, and a hurt friend wondering, *Where can she be?* You have every right to be annoyed with these girls and to say "I'm disappointed you didn't come to the party" when you see them next. If they don't apologize nicely or offer a good excuse, it may be time to start looking for some new friends.

Lost invitation?

One of my best friends is having a party. I'm sure that I should be invited, but I never got an invitation.

Left out

Option 1: Wait and see. If you're really invited, your friend may bring up the party in conversation, and it will be easy to tell her your invitation never came. **Option 2:** If other girls are talking about the party, tell them you didn't get an invitation. Word may get back to the host. **Option 3:** Ask your friend straight out: "Am I invited?" But before you do, think carefully about what you'll say if she says no.

Pushy pal

I wasn't planning to invite a certain friend to my birthday party, but she kept calling me and asking when my party was. I had no choice but to invite her.

Harassed Hostess

It was nice of you to include this girl, but in cases like this it's also O.K. to say, "I'm sorry I wasn't able to invite you to this party." The friend may get angry—disappointed girls often do. But as long as you hold on to your own temper and say what you can to heal hurt feelings, you're in the right. You owe the caller kindness, politeness, and respect. You don't owe her an invitation.

Party Pitfalls

Parties can celebrate friendships. They can also destroy them. How good are *you* at avoiding disaster? Answer these questions and find out.

Godzilla guests

How do you handle guests who threaten to ruin your party?

1. The pizzas arrive, and Cindy and Layla start **fighting** again.

a. You take a slice and listen.

b. You take sides and join in: "Oh, yes you did—"

c. You say, "Cindy, Layla. Your fighting is wrecking my party. Please stop."

2. You've had a snack, and now, as the invitations said, you're all going roller-blading. **"No way,"** says Justine. "I hate skating. I want to shoot baskets."

a. You say, "O.K. Basketball it is."

b. You yell, "Don't be a jerk. It's *my* party, and we're going to do what I want."

c. You say, "We all have our skates, and I want to go to the park as planned. Maybe we can play something else later."

3. Carol is totally **out of control.** She's slamming into other people on her skates and wrecking everything.

a. You take off your skates and cry. It's hopeless.

b. You push her into a bush. Ha! Serves her right.

c. You say, "Carol, you're hurting people. Please stop being so crazy."

4. You're in your sleeping bags and **angry** voices rise. Yes, it's Cindy and Layla—at it *again*.

a. You pull the covers over your head and wish you'd never had this party.

b. You scream, "Stop it, stop it, stop it!" till the cat hides under the sofa, then burst into tears.

c. You go get your mom. It's time for an adult to step in and call a halt.

Answers
Doormat

If you checked lots of (a)s, you let rude guests take over. Don't. A guest is supposed to arrive with good spirits, ready to do whatever she can to make the party a success. She's in the wrong if she fights, tries to run the show, or gets so wild others can't have fun. When you have a guest like this, stand up for yourself and tell her to stop. You'll have more fun—and so will the other girls at your party.

Hothead

If you checked lots of (b)s, you need to work on controlling your temper. Problem guests can be incredibly frustrating. But what happens if you blow up? The fight gets bigger, louder, and meaner. Your party veers out of control and into a ditch.

Diplomat

If you checked mostly (c)s, you keep your cool when guests act up. You don't get involved in silly fights. You stand back and tell your friends, in an honest, direct way, that they're out of line. This is the best chance you have, short of calling in the grown-ups, for reminding a friend that she's making a mess of your party.

Are you a horrid host?

Could this be you? No—or yes?

1. You have eight guests—and two **best friends.** At dinner you say, "Alice and Tiffany, sit next to me!" Before the game you cry, "Alice and Tiffany are on *my* team." At bedtime you whisper, "Alice! Tiffany! Put your sleeping bags by mine."

☐ **yes**   ☐ **no**

2. Nadia shows up without a gift. She says she **forgot** it. Forgot it?!? For the rest of the day you let her know just what you think of *that* excuse!

☐ **yes**   ☐ **no**

3. It's your party, and that means you're **in charge.** Every girl is going to do *exactly* what you tell her to do, *exactly* when you tell her to do it. Do your guests have suggestions? Too bad! *You're* in charge here.

☐ **yes**   ☐ **no**

4. New walkie-talkies! You hand one to Alice, and the two of you have a great time whispering from different rooms. When the other girls say they're bored and **left out,** you reply, "It's not *my* fault walkie-talkies are meant for two."

☐ **yes** ☐ **no**

5. Your mom *made* you invite Karen—and *you've* made sure all your other friends know that. Now you don't hesitate to join in the laughter when one of your *real* friends makes an itty-bitty comment about Karen's hair. What's the problem? You're all just **teasing.**

☐ **yes** ☐ **no**

Answers

If you said yes more than once, you're in need of a manners makeover.

1. Playing favorites is insulting to every girl who's left out.

2. Gifts are given in friendship—not forked over as payment for an invitation. A girl shouldn't criticize a gift. She shouldn't demand one, either.

3. Don't be a dictator. Yes, you've got plans for your party, and yes, your friends should go along. But if you try to control every single little thing they do, no one's going to have fun.

4. Activities should include everybody. Period.

5. A host is responsible for the well-being of every guest. At the first sign of any teasing or petty meanness, she should speak out: "Leave her alone. That's not nice." A girl who picks on one of her own guests is guilty of the worst kind of betrayal.

Ooh!

Presents

Gifts

Gifts are a way of showing you care about another person. They're great to give and great to get.

Giving

Invitations to birthday parties, weddings, and bridal or baby showers call for a gift. The exception is when the host has written "No gifts please" on the invitation. Gifts are also a tradition for various religious holidays, including Christmas and Hanukkah.

Wrap your gifts neatly and tape a card on top, with your name and the name of the recipient. A greeting, even a simple "Happy Birthday," is nice, too.

Receiving

When you get a gift, thank the giver warmly: "Great! I'll really use this!" "How pretty!" "It's my favorite color."

If you can't find something nice to say about the gift, say something nice about the giver: "How nice of you! Thank you so much!" "It was sweet of you to think of this!"

Always write a thank-you note.

Oops!

Exchanges

If I already have a gift, should I say something or just keep quiet? I don't want to disappoint the person, but I don't need two of one thing. I wouldn't be able to return it without her knowing since I wouldn't have the receipt.

Not sure

Don't say "I've already got one" when you open the gift. Talk with your parents later. If the gift came from a relative, your folks may say it's O.K. to tell the giver it's a duplicate. Most people would rather have you exchange a gift than have it end up in the bottom of a drawer. Too, see if the gift has a tag that tells you where it came from. Many stores will make exchanges without a receipt.

Your own money

Should I shop for my family myself? I have always let my parents buy something and just say on the tag that it's from me, but I'm not so sure that it's right since I'm older now.

Ashley

If you have enough money to buy things for yourself—treats, CDs, clothes, accessories, the occasional toy—then the answer is yes. It's probably time that you start saving some of your allowance and other earnings to spend on gifts for the people in your immediate family. A gift that you picked out and paid for yourself will mean ten times more to the person who gets it—and ten times more to you. The gifts don't have to be fancy. In fact, you could decide to make something and spend your money on materials. Homemade gifts are often the most wonderful gifts of all.

How much to spend

How much should I spend on friends' birthday gifts? I don't want people to think I don't have money, but I don't want to be broke, either.

Puzzled

Ideally, you'd spend roughly the same amount on your friends as they spend on you. So think about three gifts you got from friends for your last birthday. Look in the stores to see how much they cost. Figure out an average amount and make that your budget when you shop. What about wealthy friends who spent more on you than you can afford? It's O.K. to spend an average amount on them, too.

Empty-handed

One time a friend gave me the most adorable little teddy bear as a Christmas present. This came as a surprise, and I had no gift for her in return. I made the day, though, by saying lots of thank-yous and taking the bear with me everywhere!

Allison

Clever you! When you're caught empty-handed, it's even more important than usual to let the giver know that you appreciate the gift. Follow that up with a nice thank-you note—and maybe even an invitation to do something special—and you're telling your friend what she needs to know: You don't take her for granted. You care about her and are grateful for her kindness.

Thank-yous

A gift requires a thank-you note. This may seem like an ordeal, especially right after your birthday or a big holiday, but a sloppy note—or, worse, no note at all—will cause hurt feelings. Luckily, writing a nice thank-you is not only easy, it can even be fun.

Paper

Start with a fresh piece of paper or stationery. Has the dog been chewing on the notepad? Is there a grocery list on the back? Use something else.

Talk

Talk about the gift for several sentences. Have you used it? Did someone else comment on it? Are there things about it that you particularly like?

Neatness & accuracy

Write carefully. Reread what you've written. Sloppy handwriting and misspelled words tell Aunt Margo, "Boy, I can't *wait* to get this note over with!"

Friday

Dear Aunt Margo,

Thanks a lot for the sweater. I wore it to school on Tuesday and got a lot of compliments. Snails are the best! Who would have thought to put

How are you and Uncle Mort! Has he finished the doghouse he was building for Bullwrinkle?

Dad has been elected secretary of the Iris Society. Mom got her cast off. Her leg is better, but she still walks with a limp. She says hi.

Thanks again for the great sweater. I'll really enjoy it.

Love,
Kymie

Ask

Ask some questions about the person to whom you're writing. What's going on at her house? Show that you care about her.

Report

What's the news at your home? Bring Aunt Margo up to date on a thing or two.

Say "thanks" again

Mention the gift a second time, just before you end.

Oops!

Fill in the blanks

Is it polite to send the same thank-you card to everyone and just fill the person's name in the blank?

Lucy

No. A fill-in-the-blank thank-you makes the person who gets it feel like a fill-in-the-blank friend. It's far better to write a real note to everyone. You can repeat some sentences from one note to the next, but you should also have some lines that are specially written for this gift and this giver.

Teeny gifts

Do you always have to send a thank-you? If someone gives you a candy cane, do you send her a thank-you?

Jill

Presents always deserve a thank-you note. The question is, if somebody hands you a candy cane, is that a "present"? Well, yes and no. If the item you're given is inexpensive, unwrapped, and given to you casually, then it's not a formal gift, and a warm, spoken "Thank you!" may be enough. If you have any doubt about whether a written thank-you is called for, ask your mom or dad.

Unappreciated gifts

If I give someone a gift and she doesn't say thank you or even smile at me, how should I feel? I'm upset that I've disappointed her.

Tracy

A gift is a way of showing affection for another person. Does the person who gets a gift EVER have the right to turn up her nose at that? No. If you buy a gift you think a friend would like, you've done your part. So how should you feel if your friend is ungrateful? Disappointed in *her*.

Spoken vs. written

Do you always have to write your thank-yous? How about saying thank you when you see the person, or calling them on the phone? This way you can tell them more than you could on a piece of paper.

Just Wondering

Saying thank you on the phone is a great idea, but can it replace a written thank-you? For people outside your family, no. Even if your friends are sitting around you when you're opening gifts at a birthday, it's best to follow up that hurried spoken thank-you with a note. As for gifts from family members, traditions vary. In some families, if you have the chance to say thanks in person or call to say thanks on the phone, that's enough. In others, thank-yous are exchanged as faithfully as gifts. There's one rule you can count on: it's safer to write the note than to skip it.

Yum!

Eating In, Eating Out

Table Manners

People need more than good food to enjoy a meal. They also need good company. That's where table manners come in. Table manners remind us how to share, how to be considerate—not to mention how to avoid grossing out other people. They make mealtimes more pleasant at home. Your table manners are also one of the first things people will notice when you're a guest.

Simple place settings

When you set the table, do the results look like this? Good going. Is the knife blade always turned toward the plate? Bingo!

Be on time

A girl who shows up late to dinner is telling everyone else "You aren't important to me." If that's not what she means to say, she has to turn off the TV—however hard that is!—and come when she's called.

Get in the spirit

Talk. C'mon! It's friendly. "What did you do today, Dad?" "Did your pal Weevil show up at basketball practice, Norman?" "Was that nice substitute teacher at school again, Meg?" Ask questions. Get things going! Talk adds more zip to the meal than a bottle of hot sauce. (Need we add: no television, no radio, no phone calls, no books.)

Sitting

Sitting sideways, leaning back, and twisting around in your seat are like putting a sign on your chest that says "I'm bored. Get me out of here!" When you're eating, scoot in your chair and sit up straight.

Napkins

Riddle: How is a napkin like an adorable puppy? Answer: The proper place for both is in your lap.

Wait to begin

Don't start eating until everyone sits down—and that includes whoever did the cooking.

When you're a guest, watch the host. When she begins, so can you.

Guess what happened at school today?

Let's eat, everyone!

Cutting your meat

Hold your knife and fork like this.
(Don't hold them in your fists.)
Cut one (small) piece at
a time and set your knife
on the plate as you eat.

Passing

Food is passed to the right.
If you send something the
wrong way, two platters
are going to end up nose
to nose like cars mixed up
on a one-way street. If it's
a big dish, help the next
person by holding it while
he serves himself.

Don't take more than your share!

Helping yourself

Take the portion nearest
you. Leave the utensils neatly
together, handles out, so the
next person can serve herself
without fishing through the
sauce to get to them.

Chewing

Squishy sounds + the sight of chewed-up food = disgusting. That's why you should chew with your mouth closed and avoid talking while you're doing it.

Reaching

If for some reason a dish didn't get to you, ask for it: "Please pass the rolls." If you reach across the table, your elbow may end up in your pa's peas.

At rest

If you've stopped eating for a minute, position your silverware like this. At a restaurant or fancy dinner, this tells the server that you've paused, but you're not finished.

Second helpings

At home, once everybody has been served it's O.K. to ask for second helpings. If you're a guest in someone else's home, however, you should hold off. If there's enough food for seconds, the hosts will offer it.

Acting goofy

Blowing bubbles in your milk or making a castle of your mashed potatoes tells the cook you'd rather play with the food than eat it. Does the average cook appreciate this? Nope.

Elbows

So why *do* elbows have to be off the table while you eat, anyway? Because if they're on the table you look lazy and bored.

Oops!

Bugs, UFOs—it's a happy guest who knows how to handle herself in all sorts of difficult situations.

Anchovies

There are anchovies in the salad. Gug! As far as you're concerned, anchovies are the yuckiest things on the planet. It's O.K. to eat around bits of food you dislike, as long as you don't sort your food into little piles as you do it. And what if a platter comes along with food you don't want? Say a nice "No thank you."

Teeth

Uh-oh. What's this? A piece of spinach is wedged between your teeth. Say "May I be excused for a moment, please?" Go to the bathroom and do whatever you need to do to get the spinach out. (If you see something stuck in your friend's teeth, don't sit there wondering when she'll notice it herself. Let her know with a small hand motion.)

Fork

Ping! Your fork just hit the floor. If you're at a restaurant, leave the fork on the floor and ask the server for a new one. If you're at a friend's, pick up the fork and say, "Excuse me, I dropped my fork." That's the host's cue to get you a new one.

Bug

You poke your salad and a bug crawls out. Say "May I have another salad?" Explain why if the host asks. Try—really try—not to squeal and make a fuss.

Spills

Ack! Your milk topples over onto the tablecloth. **Say "I'm so sorry!" and help clean up. Try not to cry. Accidents happen to everybody—including adults.**

Achoo!

You have to sneeze. NOW! **Cover your mouth and nose with your napkin. Then if you have to blow your nose, excuse yourself. Head for the bathroom, get a tissue, and blow your nose there.**

Bathroom

The moment the host has filled your plate you realize you really, *really* have to go to the bathroom. **Say "May I be excused for a moment, please?"**

Gristle

You took a bite of meat five minutes ago and are still chewing, trying to get rid of the gristle. **Quietly take the gristle out of your mouth with your thumb and forefinger and place it on the edge of your plate.**

UFO

There's a UFO on your plate—an Unidentified Food Object. What is it? How do you eat it? You have no idea! **Keep chatting. Wait to see what the host does with the UFO on *her* plate.**

Allergic

The host appears with a platter of deviled eggs. You're allergic to eggs. **Say "No thank you. I'm allergic to eggs." Make a meal of the other foods on the table.**

Fancy Dinners

Going to a formal dinner? Lucky you! At elegant meals, the food isn't served all at once. Instead, foods are brought out, you eat them, and then they're removed and replaced with something else. Each part of the dinner is called a course. A super-duperly fancy dinner can have five courses or more—and a menu that lists them. Don't take huge portions, and try everything. (It's O.K. if you don't eat everything on your plate.)

The first course
is usually a soup or an appetizer.

The second course
might be seafood.

The third course
is the main dish or entrée (ON-tray) and the vegetables that go with it.

Salad may be served
either before or after the main course.

Dessert
Enough said. Umm!

Surprise! Sweets,
like chocolate candies, can follow dessert.

Dinner

In honor of
Mrs. Puff Pigeon's
60th Birthday

Mushroom soup

Salmon with dill sauce

Pork roast
Wild rice
Acorn squash

Green salad

Key lime pie

Bonbons

Fancy place settings

Each course requires its own silverware. In fact, there are special pieces of silverware designed for special courses.

Fish knives! Oyster forks! Depending on what's being served, a fancy place setting might look something like this:

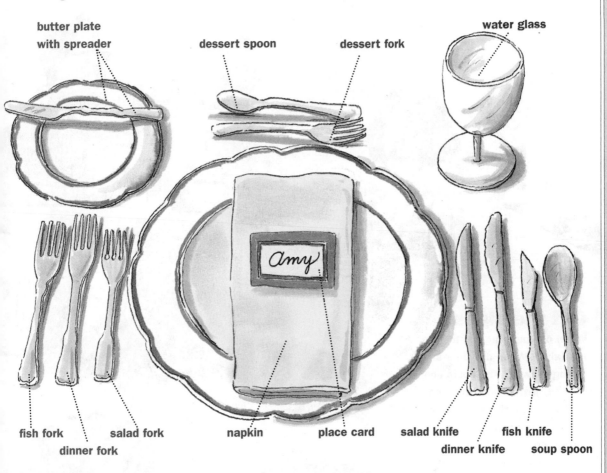

butter plate with spreader

dessert spoon

dessert fork

water glass

fish fork

dinner fork

salad fork

napkin

place card

salad knife

dinner knife

fish knife

soup spoon

Secret tip

Even more silverware may appear from the kitchen as the meal goes on. It can all get pretty confusing. But just follow what the host is doing, and remember this little secret: the silverware for the food that's served *first* is placed *farthest* from the plate. So no matter how many forks are lined up, relax. All you need to do is pick the one on the outside.

More than one girl has found herself at a fancy dinner on the other side of the kitchen door—helping out. From the kitchen, a fussy dinner seems a little like a play. Before the curtain goes up, check the table to be sure everything's ready. Then the guests appear—and the show begins!

Get the signs

When do you bring the food to the table? When do you start taking it away? The hosts can tell you, with a word or a nod of the head. If there's a guest of honor, he or she is usually sitting on the male host's right. This person is served first.

Plates on

Serve from the guest's left.
If you're holding a serving
dish, be sure the utensils
are handy and the dish is
low enough to reach.

Plates off

Remove used plates from the
right. Don't stack them at the
table. It's awkward, noisy,
messy—and v-e-r-y risky for
fancy dishes. But do scrape and
stack plates once you get to the
kitchen.

Go right

Move to the right as you circle
the table when you're serving.

Go pro

If you get good enough, you
and your pals can send flyers
to adults you know: "Formal
dinners served by experienced
waitstaff. Cleanup and big
smiles included."

Restaurants

Arriving

In a nice restaurant, diners are led to their table by a hostess or maître d' (MAY-truh DEE)— a French term for headwaiter. You're on parade in front of the other diners, so stand tall and walk briskly. It's not a good time to fight with your sister about who gets which seat.

Ordering

If you don't see anything you want on the menu, look again. Maybe they *don't* have what you were hoping for. Maybe some choices *do* sound ultra iggy. But can you find some plain chicken? A simple pasta? Restaurants serve only what's on the menu, so a wise girl is flexible when she walks in the door.

When it's your turn to speak, the waitress will look at you. Look back and talk clearly, so she knows you want the sherbet and not the sheep brains.

Tabletops

You're in charge of eating your food. The waitstaff is in charge of the tabletop. Don't rearrange things. If somebody's going to play with the candle, be sure it's not you.

Noise

Each table is supposed to be an island. Nothing going on at one table should affect what's going on at the next. It's nix on loud talking, loud laughing, bumping chairs, and flying sugar packets.

Traffic

Those trays are every bit as heavy and tippy as they look. So don't block the path between tables on your way to check out the fish tank.

Nibbling Nicely

Appetizers

Appetizers are little snacks served before guests begin the meal. Usually, you pluck them off a platter with your fingers or a toothpick, using a napkin for a plate. Some appetizers sit on tiny fluted papers. If so, take the paper with the food.

Dips and chips may also appear. All these things are meant to be shared, which is why a good guest won't re-dip a chip that's already been in her mouth. Nor will she eat all the shrimp balls—*sigh!*—no matter how much she loves them.

Part of your job as a nibbler is keeping the platter looking nice. This means taking care of your trash. Often there is a second plate or bowl near the appetizer tray to hold used toothpicks, shrimp shells, olive pits, radish stubs, papers, or whatever else you might wind up with. If there isn't such a dish, keep your trash in the napkin in your hand till you find a wastebasket. Can you "forget" the napkin on a table or park it in a potted plant? Don't even think about it.

Finger Food?

The list of foods you *shouldn't* pick up is pretty long and pretty obvious. (When's the last time you wondered if you could hold your lasagna?) But there are other foods about which you may not be so sure.

Asparagus

Believe it or not, asparagus may be eaten with the fingers if it's firm. If it's limp and dripping with sauce, go for your fork.

Bananas, bacon, & pickles

At home, you can eat these foods with your fingers. If you're in a fancy setting, use a knife and fork.

Fried chicken

When it comes to fried chicken, do as the host is doing. If she picks up her drumstick, you can pick up yours. If she uses her knife and fork, you should do the same.

Go ahead

The following foods are finger food no matter where you find them: artichokes, grapes, hamburgers, hot dogs, pizza, sandwiches, and tortillas.

Tacos

Use your hands to start, then switch to your fork to pick up the droppings.

Watermelon

If it's cubed, use your fork. If it's sliced, chances are good you're on a picnic, in which case you're free to pick it up. (Just check with your mom before you start spitting seeds at your little sister.)

Problem Foods

Soup

Insert your spoon at the edge of the bowl closest to you and move it away from you as you scoop up your soup. If you rest between sips, park the spoon on the soup plate, not in the bowl. Don't sl-l-l-urp!

Salad

Cut the lettuce into small pieces before you try to eat it. Jamming big leaves into your mouth works, but it isn't pretty. And watch out for cherry tomatoes. If you eat them whole, they squirt!

Peas

Use your knife—not your fingers—to get peas and other runaway foods onto your fork. Or you can push them up against a backstop, like a baked potato, till they roll onto your fork.

Shish kebabs

Take the blunt end of the skewer in one hand and your fork in the other. Point the tip of the skewer downward and use your fork to slide the meat and vegetables onto your plate, one chunk at a time.

Lobster

A whole lobster is served with a nutcracker. Use the nutcracker to break open the shell, and then dig out the meat with a pick or little fork.

Spaghetti

Wind spaghetti onto your fork like a ball of string. Stop before you get too much. (A few strands are all you need.)

Bread & rolls

Your roll goes on the little plate to the left of your dinner plate. Break off one bite at a time. What do you use to spread the butter? Why, that cute little butter spreader on your bread plate, of course.

All Done

Can you tell much about a girl's manners by looking at the place where she sat? You bet!

Everything was yummy!

Compliment the cook on the food and ask to be excused before you leave the table.

Push in your chair.

Take your plate to the kitchen if you're home or at a friend's. Pitch in and help clean up.

Leave your silverware positioned like this. (At a restaurant or a fancy dinner, this says to the waiter, "You can take my plate. I'm done!")

Fold your napkin and put it back on the table. If there are napkin rings, roll up the napkin and slide it back into the ring.

Let's Go!

Out and About

Neighborhoods

No matter where you live, you're part of a community. In fact, you're part of a lot of communities: a neighborhood, a city, a state, a country, a world. You have manners you use with people you know and care for. When you leave your home, take them with you.

1. You know what it feels like when your sister leaves a mess for you to clean up. Bear that in mind when you're walking the dog or deciding what to do with an empty soda can. Pick up after your pet, and hold on to all trash until you find a trash can.

2. It may be O.K. to cross the Frabbles' yard on the way to school, but it's not O.K. to play there as if it were your own. Respect others' territory.

3. *BOOM-da-BOOM-da-BOOM.* You may love that music, but there's simply no way for you to listen to it loud without making your neighbors listen to it, too.

4. You may hardly notice your bike tracks on Mr. Ott's lawn, but he may notice them—a lot. The rule is: if something is going to hurt your neighbor's property in *any* way, don't do it.

5. Good neighbors pitch in. Help old Mr. Prunepit drag his trash to the curb. Do some peer tutoring and help little Sara Spigot learn to read. Join an organization that fights drugs and crime—or that sponsors food drives or visits to nursing homes. This is your town. Don't sit by when people need help.

6. The neighbors like cars, your family likes trucks. They dress one way, you all dress another. Maybe they're of a different race, and a different religion, too. Many of the most terrible events in human history began with people who looked over the fence at their neighbors and thought, *They're different from me. They shouldn't be like that.* That's bosh. Living with different people makes life more interesting. Keep your eyes clear and your mind open.

Malls

You've got some money. You've got a ride. You've got some friends. For the next two hours, you and your pals are on your own at the mall. What now? Here are some tips and quotes from girls like you about what's right.

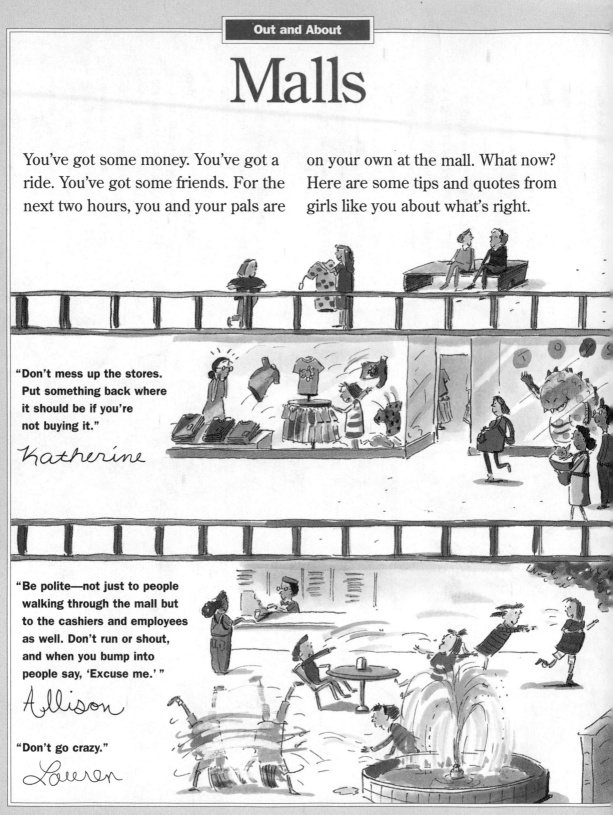

"Don't mess up the stores. Put something back where it should be if you're not buying it."

Katherine

"Be polite—not just to people walking through the mall but to the cashiers and employees as well. Don't run or shout, and when you bump into people say, 'Excuse me.'"

Allison

"Don't go crazy."

Lauren

"Be careful about taking up the whole aisle. There are lots of people with strollers and big bags who need to get by."

Ashley

Elevators

Let people get off before you try to get in. If there are older people or parents with babies waiting, hold the door and let them on first.

Getting off an elevator, the people closest to the door go first. If you're near the "door open" button in a crowded elevator, it's nice to push it while people get off.

Doors

Hold doors open for older people, people carrying packages, parents with babies, and other people who look as if they could use a hand.

Saying "Thanks" is a way to return the kindness when someone holds a door for you.

Letting a door fall back on the person coming in behind you is inconsiderate. So is goofing around with revolving doors or doors that open automatically.

Some doors love to slam shut with a bang. Try not to let them do it.

Escalators

A girl who's just remembered that she left her wallet in a changing room at the other end of the mall may brush past other people—if she says, "Excuse me, please." The rest of us should stand quietly and wait.

Movies

It's common sense—you don't want to sit near a person who's going to ruin the movie for you. Be sure you don't ruin the movie for someone else, either.

Lines

It's O.K. to save a place in line for a person who is parking the car or meeting you at the theater, or for someone who was standing with you but had to leave for a moment.

It's not O.K. if you and a pal go to the movies, see a kid you know, and say, "Hey, can we stand with you?"

Wait your turn!

Coming Soon

Hey, can we stand with you?

42

"When you go to a movie with your friends, you shouldn't be noisy. You can talk about your favorite parts *after* the movie."

Sara Beth

"Don't throw food at people or make fun of people."

Diana

"Try not to block anyone's view."

Katherine

"Be neat with food. I hate it when I go to a movie and find popcorn on the floor."

Allison

"Worst of all is when people put their feet on your chair. Don't do it!"

Ashley

"Don't hog the popcorn."

Courtney

Oops!

When you're dealing with strangers, caution comes before anything else.

Internet

You're on the Internet, chatting with someone named Meg. "I think we could be friends," she writes. "Tell me about yourself. What's your name? Where do you go to school? Maybe we could get together!"

When you're online, there's simply no way to know for sure whom you're talking to. It's possible for someone to pretend to be a girl when he's not. It's also possible for someone to pretend she's nice when she's not. So no matter how friendly you feel toward Meg, don't give out your last name, your address or phone number, or the name of your school. If she persists, leave the chat room and talk to your parents about what happened. An incident like this should be reported to the people who run the chat room, and your mom or dad can help you figure out how to do that.

At the bus stop

You're at the bus stop with your friends on a busy Saturday. A teenager walks up. He studies the bus map, turns to you, and asks, "Does this bus go to 17th Street?"

It's a reasonable question. If you know, tell him. If you don't, say, "Sorry, I don't know." It's always good to be careful, but you have friends with you, you're in a public area visible to passersby, and so far this guy is more interested in the map than he is in you. Until he does something more worrisome, you can accept a simple question as just that.

Chitchat

You're buying another CD. The man at the register says, "Back again, I see. You must really love music. What's your name? Do you live nearby?"

A little chitchat is natural with strangers to whom you have a reason to talk—a store clerk, a librarian, a bus driver. But these conversations should be brief and stick to subjects like your favorite band or a new book. They should never be personal. So tell this clerk, "Yes, I love music," but say nothing about your name or where you live or go to school. If he asks again, it's a bad sign. Leave the store, tell your parents what happened, and start buying your music someplace else.

"STOP IT!"

A boy is standing alone on the walk. He goes to your school, but he's two grades ahead. As you pass, he grabs you on the bottom.

Never worry about being polite if someone touches you in any way that feels uncomfortable. Yell "STOP IT!" and yell it LOUD. Hit him if you need to in order to get away. If he doesn't back off—if he follows you or threatens you in any way—get help from a nearby adult or run to a familiar house or a business. Tell your parents about the incident, and make sure the school knows, too.

Trust your instincts

A woman starts talking to you in the bathroom at the movies. She gives you an icky feeling. When you turn to go, she says, "Wait. Don't be rude."

Red light! "Be nice." "Be polite." "Don't be rude." These are phrases people can use to try to trick kids into bad situations. *Anyone who tries to stop you from walking away is trouble.* Trust your instincts. Get out of there. No words are needed.

Good Sports

Winners

Let their playing do the talking for them.

Don't get mad when things go against them.

Accept the ref's decisions without comment.

Don't show off when they score.

Shake hands at the end with their opponents.

Congratulate one another on their good play.

Losers

Taunt and swear at other players.

Trade accusations and excuses when they fall behind.

Argue calls with the referee.

Prance and brag after scoring.

Walk away afterward without a word to their opponents.

Blame one another for everything that goes wrong.

In the stands

Stand for "The Star-Spangled Banner" and all other national anthems. Face the flag and take off your hat.

Cheer *for* your favorite team. Do *not* taunt the competition or use words that make a sporting event sound like a war. No booing. No jeering. These athletes are playing a game. That doesn't give other people the right to insult them.

The Great Outdoors

You and the family climb into the car—and you're off. Maybe you're going to a national park a thousand miles away. Maybe you're headed to the local lake for a picnic. Either way, when you climb out, you're going to be a visitor—a tourist, a guest. How are you going to behave? Consider what you would do in the following situations. Be honest!

1. You're walking along a wooded trail when you spot a patch of flowers. They're so pretty! They're so interesting! A **sign** at the trailhead forbade picking plants, but surely it's O.K. if you take just one. You do.

a. Yes, that's me.　　　**b.** I might do this.　　　**c.** I'd never do this.

2. You buy a candy bar from the vending machine at the rest stop and eat it on the way back to the car. There's no trash can nearby. *Oh, well,* you think, *it's just one* **wrapper.** *Look at all the stuff other people have dropped around here.* You drop the wrapper.

a. Yes, that's me.　　　**b.** I might do this.　　　**c.** I'd never do this.

3. Woo! So this is the Grand Canyon. It's so big! There's a sign telling people not to throw things over the edge because it's **unsafe** for those below. Still, you wonder. . . . No one's watching, so you pick up a rock and pitch it.

a. Yes, that's me.　　　**b.** I might do this.　　　**c.** I'd never do this.

4. You and your friend are walking along the lake when you see it: a bird's nest hiding in the reeds. It's the tiniest little thing with such pretty **eggs.** It would look great on your dresser at home. You pick it up.

a. Yes, that's me.   **b.** I might do this.   **c.** I'd never do this.

5. The guide says that these Indian ruins have been here for 800 years. Your friend whispers, "Let's carve our **initials** in this rock to show we were here, too." You do it.

a. Yes, that's me.   **b.** I might do this.   **c.** I'd never do this.

6. You're at the beach with your pals—and several thousand other folks. "I brought my **radio,**" you say. "Let's listen to some music." You turn it on, and the volume up. *Way* up.

a. Yes, that's me.   **b.** I might do this.   **c.** I'd never do this.

Answers
Natural disaster
If you had more than one (a), you should take a long, hard look at yourself before you leave the house. You put yourself before other people, treasured monuments, and the environment. You leave a place worse off than it was before you came—and that's a shameful thing.

"Hello, this is your conscience speaking"
If you had mostly (b)s, you know what's right but are too easily tempted to act selfishly. You can do better!

Invisible girl
If you had mostly (c)s, you're aces in open spaces. You know that when it comes to nature, a girl should enjoy it without leaving a trace that she was ever there.

Thanks!

Faraway Lands

Pretend you're in another country.
Which questions would be considered
rude?

Answer

All of them are rude!

There isn't a place on the planet where people don't take natural pride in their customs, religions, language, and history. If you behave as if the American way is the *only* way, it's just plain insulting. Want proof? Then reread these questions, and consider how you would feel if a visitor to this country said the same things to *you.*

Yikes!

Horrors

Oops!

There are some things that make a girl cringe, and horribly humiliating moments are among them. What *do* you do when you're so embarrassed you could die?

Unwanted

A bunch of girls you know are at the pool, and you decide to join them. You're spreading out your towel when Miranda leans over and says, "This is Hannah's birthday party."

You can't crash a party. The question is how to leave without showing the pain and embarrassment you feel. It's going to be hard, but try to pretend this is no big deal. Say "Whoops! I didn't know. Have fun, everybody." Then find a private place where you can recover.

Accident

Crash! You've dropped your drink. The glass shatters and juice sprays all over Mrs. Angelini's white carpet.

Tell Mrs. Angelini how sorry you are, and do everything—*everything*—you can to help clean up. Say you're sorry again when you leave, and let your parents know about the spill once you get home. They may want to talk to Mrs. Angelini, too, and perhaps hire a carpet cleaner. Accidents happen—that's just the way it is. If you apologize sincerely and do what you can to put things right, most people will forgive you.

Forgot

You're on your bike when the thought suddenly hits you. Sarah's party! It was today! You said you'd go and you totally forgot!

Go home, call Sarah, and apologize: "Sarah, I'm so sorry! I forgot about your party. I was looking forward to it, too. I hope my not being there didn't wreck anything. Please forgive me!" Let Sarah be mad at you without getting mad back. Deliver her gift as soon as possible, and include a note apologizing again.

Wetting your pants

You're having lunch at Debbie's. She is *so* funny! You laugh and laugh and— OOOH NOOO! You just wet your pants!

Honesty and humor are the only defense against embarrassment as crushing as this. So say what you're thinking: "This is the most embarrassing thing that's ever happened to me in my whole life." If you can make a joke, that's even better ("I'm going to change my name and move to New Zealand"). Apologize for the mess, clean it up yourself, and accept a change of clothes if it's offered. At that point, Debbie and her family will probably let the subject drop, and so can you.

Gross

Gross behavior is another thing that can make a girl say "Yikes!" It usually has to do with something unsanitary and unsightly that people do with their bodies. Watching somebody bite her nails is a little gross. Watching somebody pick her nose is *really* gross. It turns your stomach because you know that some slippery sludge might end up on a pencil that you pick up later. It's unclean and . . . well, *gross*.

Nose-picking

Please! If you have to pinch, poke, or prod your body, do so behind the bathroom door.

Gum

Keep your gum to yourself. Chew it quietly and find a trash can when you're done. On the ground or stuck under a counter, your wad is a disgusting surprise for someone else.

Sneezing

Cover your mouth and nose with your hand so you don't spray saliva, mucus, and germs on everyone nearby.

Burping

Burping on purpose is popular with toddlers and kids who are desperate for a laugh. The rest of us burp only when we have to, and as quietly as we can.

"Excuse me" is the right thing to say if you make noise when you burp. If somebody else burps, the right thing to say is nothing.

Washing

Bathe often and keep your face, hands, and hair clean. Greasy hair is unattractive, and body odor makes others want to get as far away from you as they can.

Smirking

We all make unpleasant smells and noises sometimes. We can't help it. Making a big fuss when somebody passes gas—by grinning, holding your nose, rolling your eyes, or saying "P.U."—amounts to teasing. The real stink in the room comes from the smirker's manners.

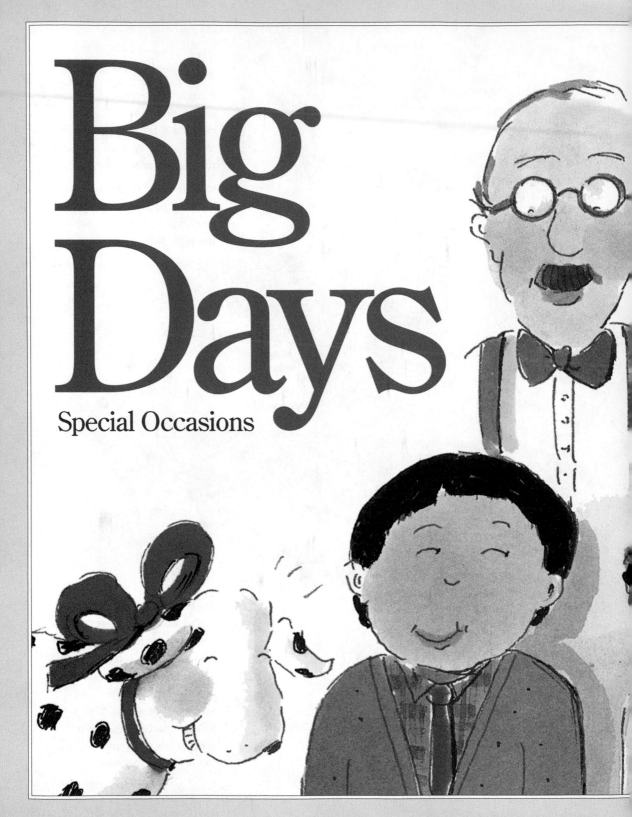

Big
Days

Special Occasions

Family Gatherings

Extended families get together for holidays and big occasions—births, weddings, funerals, bar and bat mitzvahs, christenings, first communions, and graduations. For you, a family event may mean putting aside your own friends and activities for the day, but it's worth it. What you *really* don't want to miss are the moments and memories that bind your family together. So here are some tips for making the most of a family bash.

The **star** of the day gets the spotlight when it comes to graduations, birthdays, and so on. If you try to compete, jealousy will eat through your day like a worm through an apple.

When the **camera** comes out, smile. Making faces produces nothing but irritated relatives and lousy pictures.

Your **love** means more to older people than anything in the world. So don't be a miser. When Grandma comes in, throw your arms around her neck and give her a kiss.

Bored? Don't sit around feeling sorry for yourself. Do something about it. Grab a Frisbee and some cousins, and get something going! The one sure way to have a good time is to create one yourself.

Be patient. Big groups can't do anything fast. If you're trying to get 15 people out of the house and into the yard, it's going to take a while. Plan on it.

Traditions make for great memories. You may think it's a little goofy that your Uncle Bart always makes the whole family sing a crazy song that he and your dad made up when they were boys. But traditions are mysterious things. Once planted in your memory, they'll grow in your heart. Join in.

Let's play a game.

congratulations...

Habits differ from family to family. You may be used to eating at 5:30. Your relatives may want to eat at 7:00. You may play horseshoes one way, and your cousin Midge may play it another. If everybody insists on her own way, the visit will be a disaster. Be flexible and compromise.

Stuck at home

Every time my aunt comes to town, my family gets together. It's all fine until the little kids come. They hound me! I know they love me, and I love them, but I'm expected to watch them.

a girl with no social life

Families come with certain obligations, and keeping company with cousins is one of them. Still, there's no law that says you have to stay locked in the house, especially if the little kids are around for more than a day. Talk to your mom about making plans that will include friends and cousins both. Maybe you and a friend can lead the pack to the pool, the park, or a movie theater. Or maybe you can cook up a show or a moneymaking scheme that will entertain everybody—including you.

Divided family

I am almost 12 years old. At 12, I will have a celebration called a bat mitzvah. My parents are divorced, and my dad is paying for the celebration. Some of my relatives on my mom's side don't want to come. I'm closer to my mom's side than to my dad's, and I really want them to come. My aunt said we could have a special dinner together instead, but it's not the same.

Upset

Write these relatives a note telling them how you feel. A bat mitzvah is about you—about your growing up and your commitment to your religion. It has nothing to do with your parents' divorce. If these relatives stay away, the only person they're going to hurt is you. Tell them that. Tell them you love them. Then say, "This is important to me. I really want you to come."

Weddings

Weddings are as different as the people in them. They can be religious or nonreligious, indoors or outdoors, formal or informal. A traditional wedding consists of a ceremony and a reception. A girl can have a role in the wedding as a bridesmaid or flower girl. She can also attend as a guest. Either way, she wants her best manners in tow.

Guests

Wedding invitations are usually printed up specially for the event. If a girl is invited, her name will be written on the envelope.

A written R.S.V.P. is required for wedding invitations. So is a gift. Your parents will probably take care of both.

Generally, the later in the day a wedding takes place, the fancier it is. A wedding designated "black tie" or "white tie" is very fancy indeed. Keep this in mind when you're deciding what to wear.

Bridesmaids

Being a bridesmaid gets you a special dress—and special responsibilities.

There is always at least one rehearsal for the members of the wedding party. That's when you find out what you'll need to do. Listen up and ask questions then, because there won't be time in the hectic moments before the start of the wedding.

Getting seated

Guests are seated by an usher—family and friends of the groom on one side of the aisle, family and friends of the bride on the other. In most Christian services, the mothers of the bride and groom are seated individually just before the ceremony starts. (That's how guests know it's about to begin.)

The bridal party

The bridal party, or wedding party, is made up of everybody who stands at the front with the bride and groom during the service. This includes the ushers and best man, who are usually brothers or good friends of the groom, and the bridesmaids, who are usually sisters or good friends of the bride. It may also include a ring bearer (a young boy who's entrusted with carrying the rings) and a flower girl (a girl age eight or younger who walks ahead of the bride).

The vows

The couple make promises about the life they will lead, reflecting the love they feel for each other. Often they exchange rings. In a Jewish wedding, the pair stands under a canopy called a *chuppah* (HUHP-pa), and the groom breaks a glass wrapped in a napkin as a reminder of the sorrows the Jewish people have experienced.

What should guests and members of the wedding party do during the ceremony? Listen quietly, of course.

The procession

The exact order in which members of the wedding party move to the front depends on both religion and preference. Usually bridesmaids and flower girls go down the aisle before the bride. The trick is not to rush it.

A girl should walk slowly—gracefully, calmly—with a smile on her face. Last of all *(ta-da!)* comes the bride, often on her father's arm. When she appears, the guests stand.

The receiving line

Members of the wedding party stand in a line while guests file past one by one. Guests should move down the line quickly, shaking hands, congratulating the bride and groom, greeting people they know, and introducing themselves to people they don't know.

A bridesmaid in the receiving line can expect to meet and greet lots and lots of people. Her job is to stay cheerful and friendly the entire time. Once all the guests have gone through the line, the members of the wedding party are free to join the reception.

108

The reception

A reception can be anything from a simple get-together in a church hall to a big sit-down dinner someplace fancy. Toasts are made to the bride and groom. (The adults often drink wine or champagne with each toast. A girl can drink juice or water.) At some point, the newlyweds cut their cake.

Often there's music and dancing. The bride and groom dance the first dance alone. After that, everyone else can join in—including you.

If someone asks you to dance and you don't want to, say, "Thanks, but I'd rather just watch." If you *do* want to dance, say O.K.—and go to it.

Would you like to dance?

Farewell

When the bride and groom are getting ready to leave, the bride tosses her bouquet into a group of unmarried women and girls. If you're included, jump like an NBA All-Star but don't push and shove like a tackle in the NFL.

As the couple make their way out, well-wishers shower them—gently!—with rice, birdseed, or confetti.

Funerals

If you've never been to a funeral, the whole idea may make you nervous. Don't be. Funerals are sad and serious occasions, but they aren't frightening. The whole point is to help comfort people who have lost someone dear to them. A funeral affirms the religious beliefs of the family. It celebrates the life of the person who died—and the love that lives on.

Behavior

Keep your voice low and behave seriously. Loud talking and laughing are insulting to the feelings of others.

At some funerals, the body of the person who's died is on display in the coffin. You don't need to approach the coffin if you don't want to. If you do pause for a moment in front of the coffin, use the time to say a short prayer or to think about the person and what he or she meant to you.

Dress

Dress nicely. You don't need to wear black, but this isn't the time to wear your wildest, brightest outfit, either.

Guest book

At many funerals there is a guest book, in which people attending the ceremony sign their name. The book is a keepsake for the family.

Receiving line

Either before or after the ceremony, there may be a receiving line, where members of the family greet other people. When you go through a receiving line, shake hands and introduce yourself. Say something about what the dead person meant to you: "Mr. Hornbeck was the best teacher I ever had. I'll always remember him."

Tears

You may see people crying; you may cry yourself. This is natural. Don't feel ashamed to let your feelings show, and don't feel alarmed if others express their grief, either.

It's a good idea to bring some tissues with you.

Home visits

There may be an informal gathering at the family's home following the funeral. Visits to the home may occur at other times as well. If the family is Christian, there may be a gathering the night before the funeral. This is called a wake. If the family is Jewish, the family may stay at home for a number of days after the funeral, a tradition called *sitting shiva*. This is also a period when friends and relatives often visit.

A home visit calls for the same kind of manners you bring to the funeral itself: quiet and respectful.

What can you say to a friend who's lost someone she loved? And what can you do that might make things easier for her? Girls who have had to deal with death have this to say about how friends can help.

I'm sorry.

"I'm sorry" is a good start

"Even if all you say is 'I'm sorry,' you should say it. You'd be surprised at how nice it feels to know that someone cares."

Emily

Write a note

"When my loved one died, I got lots of 'sorry's from kids at school. It was nice of them to think of me, but one of my friends wrote me a letter. It really made me feel that if I needed anyone to talk to, she was there for me."

Marisa

Send flowers

"When my dad died, my classmates sent me an ornament of flowers. I still have it today, and that was seven years ago."

Rachele

Take food

"If you know someone who has lost a loved one, bring her family food. Usually the family is too sad to cook."

Jessica

Dear Alex,
I'm so sorry about your dad. I loved the way he would always tell silly jokes in the car. He was so proud of you! I'll always remember him.

Love,
Sakina

Don't avoid a grieving girl

"My brother died about a year ago. My friends were kind of supportive, but some of my classmates were nervous around me and the subject of death. They avoided me. I would have felt better if they had told me they were uncomfortable. Girls should know that it's O.K. to talk about the death. Don't avoid talking about it completely, or you'll just make your friend feel worse."

Kelsey

Say you'll remember

"My father died two years ago this summer. When I went to school that year, everybody said they were sorry. One person told me she would always remember my dad. That really touched me."

Heather

Be willing to listen

"My grandfather died of cancer. When I went back to school, one of my friends said, 'I guess you don't want to talk about it.' But that wasn't true. I *did* want to talk. Often, remembering things about the person can make you feel a little less sad."

Julia

Be a friend

"When my friend's father died, I didn't know what to say. I don't really think you can know. But I learned that what my friend really needed was to know someone cared, and that if she needed support or just to talk she would always have me as a friend."

Robyn

113

Tea with the Queen

When it comes to high officials, a lot of special rules apply. These rules are called protocol. Protocol encourages respect for positions of authority—for presidents and kings, senators and judges, generals and diplomats. In places like Washington, D.C., where such people tend to get together, protocol determines things like who goes first and proper forms of address. It's nothing to be scared of. If you're invited to a fancy government event, simply ask your parents about what's expected. Add the manners you already know, and guess what? You're ready to go *anywhere*.

Just imagine . . .

Word of your marvelous manners has reached the palace.

An invitation arrives in the mail. The Queen is inviting you to tea on Thursday at 4:00.

Your friends can always count on you for a prompt R.S.V.P.— and so can the Queen. You get out your nice stationery and write a note saying that you accept with pleasure.

When the day comes, you arrive promptly (as you always do). A man meets you at the door. You stand tall, look him in the eye, and smile. "How do you do?" you say.

You're prepared

Your heart's fluttering, but you're not scared. Before you came you asked your mom a lot of questions about queens and protocol. You know the rules.

You know, for instance, that Americans really don't *have* to curtsy to royalty, but you've decided to curtsy anyway, because you're a guest at the palace and it seems like the nice thing to do. (Besides, you know how to curtsy from ballet.)

You place the toes of your right foot behind and a little to the left of your left heel. Then you bend your knees.

You are introduced—or "presented"—to the Queen. "Hello, Your Majesty," you say. From then on you know it's O.K. to call her "Ma'am" (rhymes with "ham").

"Have some tea, dear," says the Queen, and you do. (Your little sister thinks it's fancy to stick out her pinkie when she holds a teacup. You know better!)

Hello, Your Majesty.

It's a breeze

Now you can chat and enjoy yourself. And guess what? You're *good* at this. You really are! You know how to handle your food and how to sit. You can think of things to say to keep a conversation going. When the Queen drops her cookie in her tea, you know just what to say. (Nothing.) How did you become so confident and graceful? Why, from using these very same manners with your family and friends every day.